EXTREME
ADRENALINE
BMX
By Heather C. Hudak
AV2
www.av2books.com

Step 1
Go to **www.av2books.com**

Step 2
Enter this unique code
HFTANVQAP

Step 3
Explore your interactive eBook!

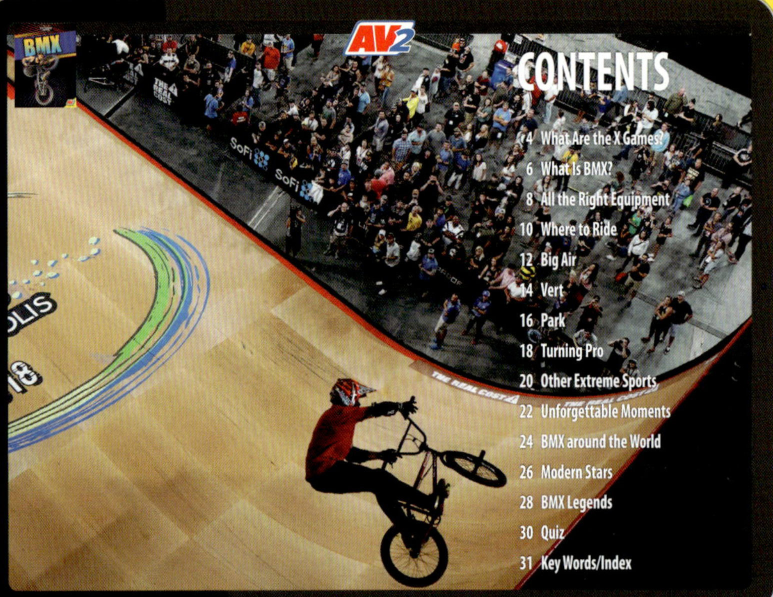

AV2 is optimized for use on any device

Your interactive eBook comes with...

Contents
Browse a live contents page to easily navigate through resources

Audio
Listen to sections of the book read aloud

Videos
Watch informative video clips

Weblinks
Gain additional information for research

Try This!
Complete activities and hands-on experiments

Key Words
Study vocabulary, and complete a matching word activity

Quizzes
Test your knowledge

Slideshows
View images and captions

... and much, much more!

BMX

CONTENTS

WHAT ARE THE X GAMES?

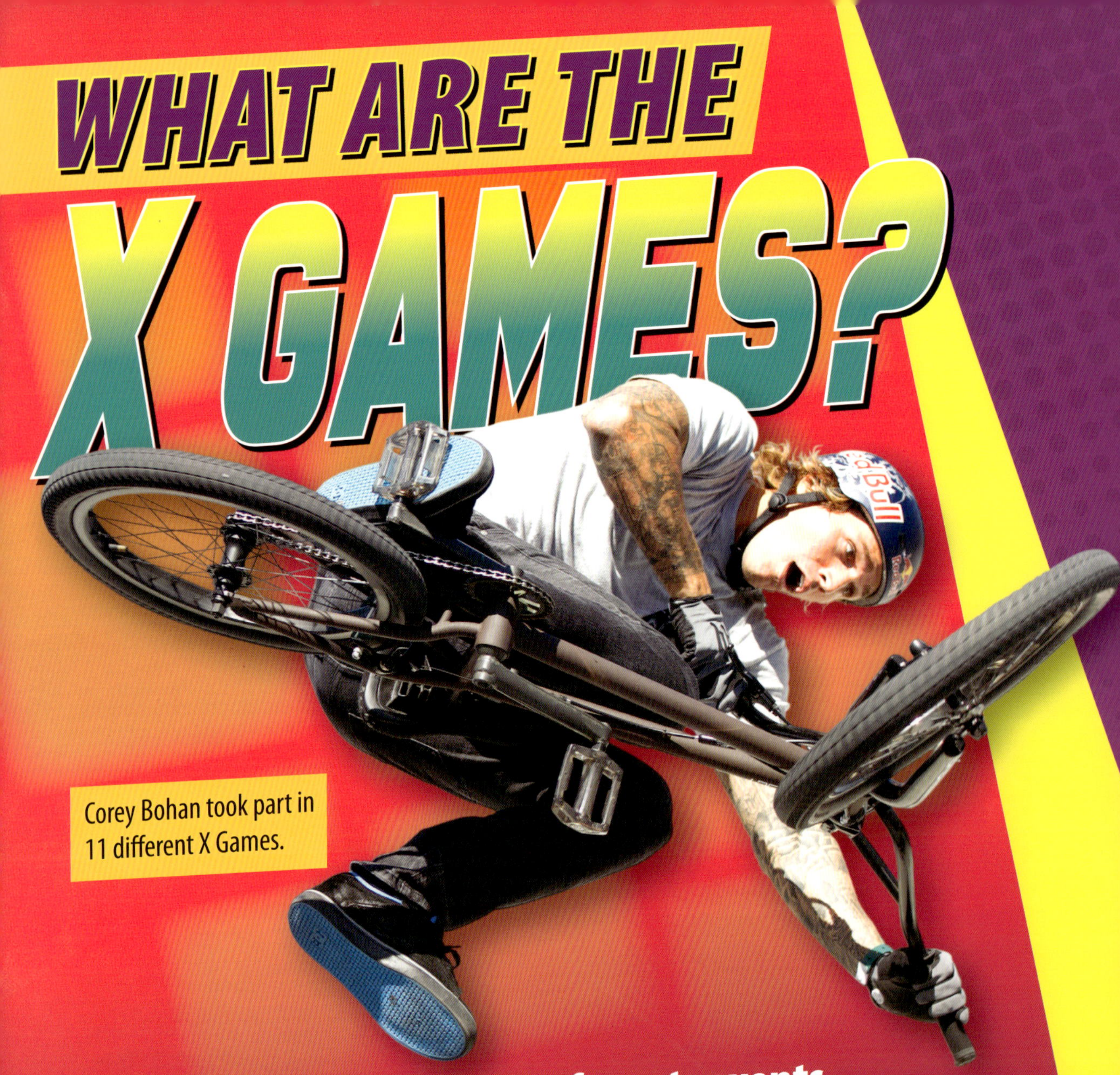

Corey Bohan took part in 11 different X Games.

The X Games are a series of sports events for the best athletes in extreme sports.

Extreme sports are done at high speeds. **Athletes** must wear special gear to help keep them safe. Events such as the X Games show off the skill and hard work of the athletes. These events also show how difficult extreme sports are.

Some of the best BMX riders in the world come to the X Games. These riders show off extreme moves in front of large crowds. X Games events have riders doing stunts in the air or racing to the finish line.

X FEST

The X Games has more than just sports. Each year, bands from all over the world play for fans at the X Games. X Fest is the name of the X Games concert. There is punk rock, hip-hop, and alternative music. The bands perform between events. They keep the crowds excited for the games.

Different bands play every day of X Fest.

Olympic Sport

BMX was officially added to the Olympics for the 2008 Beijing Summer Games.

Speed Racing

The average BMX race lasts 25 to 40 seconds.

Young Riders

In the U.S., 70 percent of BMX riders are younger than 24.

WHAT IS BMX?

BMX stands for bicycle **motocross**. Athletes ride on special bicycles that have large wheels. The bicycles have only one gear. This makes them easy to use for this style of racing.

There are several types of BMX riding. Riders speed along dirt tracks in BMX racing. The first one to the finish line wins the race. Riders perform tricks on their bikes in freestyle BMX.

There are five types of freestyle BMX. These are Street, Park, Vert, Dirt, and Flatland. Each type uses the bike in different ways and uses different features.

BMX TIMELINE

1963 The Stingray bicycle is made. Young people use it to perform tricks.

1977 The American Bicycle Association (ABA) is formed to create rules for BMX racing and tricks.

1981 The International BMX Federation is founded.

1984 Freestyle BMX becomes an official sport when the American Freestyle Association is formed.

1995 BMX events are part of the first X Games.

2008 Anne-Caroline Chausson of France wins the first Women's Cycling BMX Olympic gold medal.

2011 USA BMX is formed. It brings together the American Bicycle Association and the National Bicycle League.

2020 BMX Park is added to the Olympics at the Tokyo Summer Games.

ALL THE RIGHT EQUIPMENT

BMX freestyle riders wear shirts that let them move and pants that will not get caught on the bicycle. Riders wear shoes that give them better grip on the bike pedals.

Many BMX racers wear pants, long-sleeved shirts, and closed-toe shoes. Most riders wear special gloves so they can grip the handlebars better.

Riders must wear the proper equipment to protect themselves if they fall.

The Beginning

BMX was invented by kids who were doing motocross stunts on road bikes.

Standard Size

BMX bikes have 20-inch wheels (50.8 centimeters).

No Tangle

By using Gyros, BMX riders can spin their handlebars 360 degrees without twisting the brake cables.

Helmet

The helmet is the most important piece of safety equipment. Helmets have saved many riders from head injuries.

Knee and Elbow Pads

Many riders wear knee and elbow pads. Riders learn how to use these pads as cushions if they fall.

Bikes

Racing bikes are very light. They are meant for riding on dirt tracks. Freestyle bikes are heavier than racing bikes. These bikes need to take the force of tricks and stunts.

Wheels

Racing bikes have extra **tread**. This helps grip the dirt track and get more speed. Freestyle bikes have a smooth tread for riding on concrete.

Pegs

Riders use pegs on the **axles** to balance while doing tricks.

WHERE TO RIDE

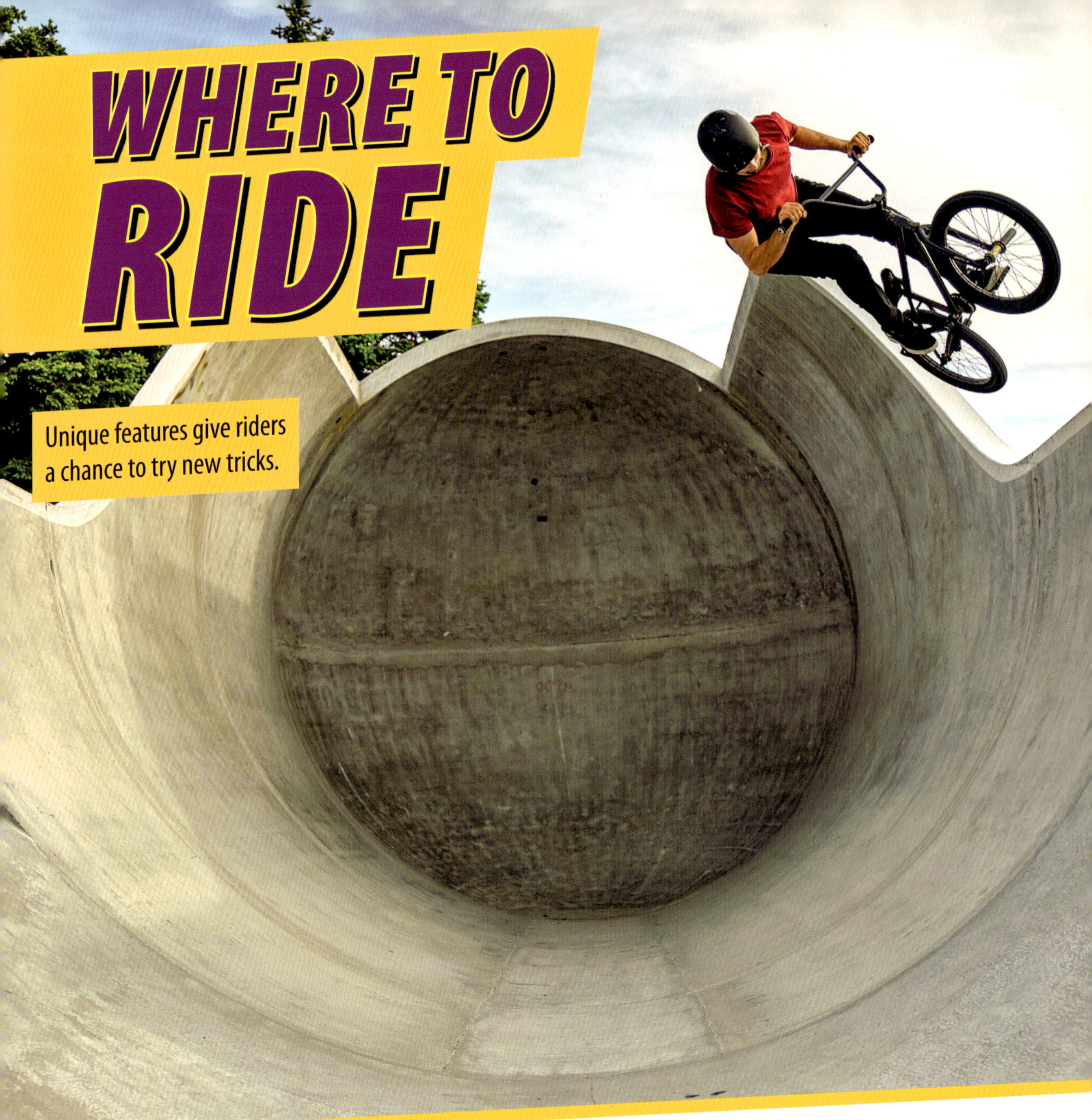

Unique features give riders a chance to try new tricks.

BMX riding can be done almost anywhere there is pavement, dirt, or wood. Many freestyle BMX riders practice at skateparks. Skateparks have features like **halfpipes** and **quarterpipes** that riders can use to perform tricks. BMX racers ride on dirt tracks that have features such as jumps and hills.

There are five BMX events at the X Games. Each takes place on a different course.

The Vert event takes place on a halfpipe that launches riders high in the air. In Park, riders use features like concrete barriers to perform tricks. The Big Air event is known for the MegaRamp. Riders can also compete in the Dirt and Street events.

Balancing tricks can be practiced wherever there is room.

BIG AIR

The Big Air height record was set at 27 feet (8.2 meters) above the quarterpipe by Kevin Robinson.

Big Air at the X Games is an exciting event. Riders face a series of ramps and jumps. First, riders take an elevator ride to the top of a MegaRamp, which has an 80-foot (24-m) drop. Riders roll down the drop and launch off a ramp at the other end. They perform a stunt before they land at the top of another ramp. Riders then speed to the top of a quarterpipe. Riders perform a trick at the top before turning around.

Douglas Oliveira is known for chasing the Big Air height record.

Eight riders take part in this event. Each rider gets four tries to earn a high score. The judges score the riders based on tricks performed over the gaps and on the quarterpipe.

The top three riders move on to the final round. Each rider has five runs in the finals. The rider with the most points wins the event.

Big Air
Past Winners

X Games Minneapolis 2019

Gold – Ryan Williams
Silver – Morgan Wade
Bronze – Vince Byron

X Games Sydney 2018

Gold – Ryan Williams
Silver – James Foster
Bronze – Mykel Larrin

VERT

Jamie Bestwick has spent his career competing in Vert. He has taken part in 26 X Games Vert competitions.

Vert, or Vertical, riders ride up one wall of a halfpipe, soar above the top, and do a trick in the air before landing. Then, they roll down the halfpipe and up the other wall. They do another trick before landing. Riders keep doing this until the end of their runs.

Francisco "Coco" Zurita is the first rider to land a triple tail-whip.

Riders get 60 seconds and three runs to show off their tricks. Their scores are based on how well the tricks were done, how hard the tricks were, how original the tricks were, and the height of the jumps.

Only eight riders go on to the final round. The rider with the highest score in the final round wins the event.

Vert Past Winners

X Games Minneapolis 2019

Gold – Vince Byron
Silver – Jamie Bestwick
Bronze – Mykel Larrin

X Games Austin 2016

Gold – Jamie Bestwick
Silver – Simon Tabron
Bronze – Dennis McCoy

PARK

Colton Walker also competes in BMX Dirt.

The Park event takes place on a special course. The course is like a skatepark. It has many features that the riders can use throughout the event. Twelve riders take part in the Park event.

Each Park rider gets two 75-second runs to show the judges their best moves. Riders can ride around the course and use the features in any way they want during their runs.

Logan Martin won gold with a score of 93.33 at the 2019 Park competition.

Some of the features on the course are ramps, quarterpipes, and rails. Common tricks riders do are **tailwhips** and **backflips**.

The more difficult the tricks performed, the higher the points scored. Six riders go on to the final round. The rider with the highest score after the final round wins the event.

Park
Past Winners

X Games Minneapolis 2019

Gold – Logan Martin
Silver – Rim Nakamura
Bronze – Jose Torres

X Games Austin 2016

Gold – Dennis Enarson
Silver – Logan Martin
Bronze – Kyle Baldock

TURNING PRO

Sponsors will put their logo on riders' equipment, such as gloves or helmets.

The first step to becoming a professional BMX rider is to get sponsored. A sponsor is a company that will pay for equipment, travel costs, and living costs while a rider is training. A sponsored rider will wear the company name or **logo** at events.

A person must be very good at BMX to be sponsored. Riders who try new tricks and stunts are more likely to get noticed. Companies will sometimes contact riders about sponsorship. Many also riders contact companies about sponsorship. X Games riders do not need to have a sponsor to go to the games.

To take part in the X Games, riders must work hard, practice new tricks, and take part in many events. People from BMX companies and the best BMX riders suggest riders for the X Games. The X Games chooses riders to invite to the games. BMX riders who have top scores at recent events can be invited. Riders who have been in the sport for a long time may also be invited to the games.

Sponsors will also help put on events so they can find new riders.

OTHER EXTREME SPORTS

BMX riding is a sport that is popular around the world. It is not the only sport where a person rides a bike. These sports are like BMX.

Motocross

Motocross riders use special motorcycles to race along tracks or do tricks and stunts. Most motocross races take place on dirt tracks that have turns and hills. Riders use ramps and other obstacles to perform tricks in freestyle motocross.

Cycling

Cycling is the oldest bicycle sport. The Tour de France is one of the biggest cycling events. The Olympics also has cycling events.

Mountain Biking

In mountain biking, people ride special bikes over rocky trails. These bikes have wide tires that grip the ground better than thin tires.

Ice Biking

In ice biking, cyclists ride on ice and snow. Ice bikers may use studded tires to help grip the slippery path.

UNFORGETTABLE MOMENTS

During the X Games, there have been many unforgettable moments. Some of these are record-breaking wins, long falls, and new tricks.

Ryan Williams made history when he did a backflip **drop-in** onto the MegaRamp at the 2019 Big Air Event in Minneapolis, Minnesota. This was the first time someone has done this trick onto the MegaRamp. It was also the first time Williams had ever done this trick. Williams exciting run earned him the gold.

On the final Big Air run at the 2015 X Games in Austin, Texas, Colton Satterfield won gold by being the first person to do a **double flair** on the MegaRamp. Kevin Robinson was the first to do the trick in the Vert event in 2006.

History was made at the 2019 X Games Vert event in Minneapolis, Minnesota. Mykel Larrin was the first person to land a triple downside tailwhip. Larrin used the trick to finish his run. Larrin won bronze for his run.

BMX AROUND THE WORLD

BMX riders travel all over the globe to visit BMX parks. Use this map and research online to discover your next BMX park. Then, answer the questions to test your knowledge.

Ray's MTB Park
Cleveland, Ohio, United States
- Offers different areas for practice and unusual tricks
- An indoor park that can be used all year

Rye Airfield
Rye, New Hampshire, United States

- Offers indoor and outdoor courses
- Home to both local pros and amateurs

SMP Skatepark
Shanghai, China
- Largest skatepark in the world
- Features the world's largest concrete bowl

Monster Skatepark
Sydney, New South Wales, Australia

- Offers tracks for both freestyle BMX riding and BMX racing
- Located in the Sydney Olympic Park

TEST YOUR KNOWLEDGE

1. Which country has the most BMX parks?
2. Where has the Summer X Games been hosted in the past three years?

X GAMES VENUES

= Summer X Games Host City

1. Newport, Rhode Island, USA
2. San Diego, California, USA
3. San Francisco, California, USA
4. Los Angeles, California, USA
5. Austin, Texas, USA
6. Minneapolis, Minnesota, USA
7. Boise, Idaho, USA
8. Mexico City, Mexico
9. Foz do Iguaçu, Brazil
10. Kuala Lumpur, Malaysia
11. Shanghai, China
12. Seoul, Korea
13. Phuket, Thailand
14. Barcelona, Spain
15. Munich, Germany
16. Sydney, Australia

MODERN STARS

GARRETT REYNOLDS

Hometown
Toms River, New Jersey, United States

Born
August 2, 1990

NOTES
- Was competing at age 12
- Has won 15 X Games medals in his career

CHAD KERLEY

Hometown
San Diego, California, United States

Born
January 27, 1994

NOTES
- Started out as a BMX racer at age 4
- Sponsored by Premium, Nike, and Dan's Comp

COLTON SATTERFIELD

Hometown
Salt Lake City, Utah, United States

Born
September 24, 1989

NOTES
- Was first interested in skateboarding
- Rides in Vert and Big Air

DAKOTA ROCHE

Hometown
Huntington Beach, California, United States

Born
July 21, 1987

NOTES
- Began riding his BMX bike on local trails at age 10
- Has filmed many popular videos of his skills in the Street discipline

BMX LEGENDS

MAT HOFFMAN

Hometown
Oklahoma City, Oklahoma, United States

Born
January 9, 1972

NOTES
- Only BMX rider to land a no-handed 900 in a competition
- Invented over 100 freestyle tricks

JAMIE BESTWICK

Hometown
Nottingham, United Kingdom

Born
July 8, 1971

NOTES
- Has won 12 X Games gold medals
- Despite his success, says that his biggest fear is heights

DAVE MIRRA

Hometown
Chittenango, New York, United States

Born
April 4, 1974

NOTES
- Held the record for most X Games medals until 2013
- Could not compete for six months because of a car accident in 1993

KEVIN ROBINSON

Hometown
Providence, Rhode Island, United States

Born
December 19, 1971

NOTES
- Was the first to land a double flair in competition
- Set the record for highest air in 2008 at 27 feet

QUIZ

1. In what year were the first X Games held?
2. What does a sponsor help BMX riders with?
3. What are the five BMX disciplines in the X Games?
4. When was the Stingray bicycle built?
5. Who won gold in the 2019 Big Air event?
6. How many riders compete in the Park event?
7. What is the most important piece of safety equipment for a BMX rider?
8. How long do runs last in the Vert competition?
9. How many inches is the diameter of a standard BMX wheel?
10. How long is the drop from the top of the MegaRamp in the Big Air event?

Answers

1. 1995
2. Paying for equipment, travel costs, and living costs
3. Big Air, Dirt, Park, Street, Vert
4. 1963
5. Ryan Williams
6. Twelve
7. A helmet
8. 60 seconds
9. 20
10. 80 feet (24 m)

KEY WORDS

athletes: people who train for and take part in sporting events

axles: cylinders that attach the wheels to the bike and allow the wheels to spin

backflips: tricks done when the rider does a backwards somersault in the air

double flair: a double backflip while spinning

drop-in: beginning to go down a ramp

halfpipes: two ramps that curve inward and are facing each other with an area of flat ground between them

logo: the symbol or image a company uses to represent itself

motocross: a sport in which specially designed motorcycles are raced on dirt and concrete tracks or used to perform tricks

quarterpipes: a ramp that curves inward with an area of flat ground between them

tailwhips: tricks done when the back end of the bike spins all the way around while the front end remains in one place

tread: the knobby rubber on a tire

INDEX

Get the best of both worlds.

AV2 bridges the gap between print and digital.

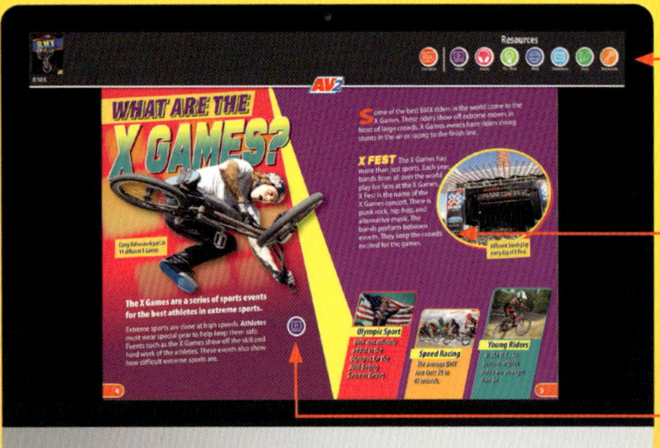

The expandable resources toolbar enables quick access to content including **videos**, **audio**, **activities**, **weblinks**, **slideshows**, **quizzes**, and **key words**.

Animated videos make static images come alive.

Resource icons on each page help readers to further **explore key concepts**.

Published by AV2
350 5th Avenue, 59th Floor
New York, NY 10118
Website: www.av2books.com

Library of Congress Control Number: 2019047760

ISBN 978-1-7911-1828-0 (hardcover)
ISBN 978-1-7911-1829-7 (softcover)
ISBN 978-1-7911-1830-3 (multi-user eBook)
ISBN 978-1-7911-1831-0 (single user eBook)

Printed in Guangzhou, China
1 2 3 4 5 6 7 8 9 0 24 23 22 21 20

032020
101319

Project Coordinator: Ryan Smith
Designer: Terry Paulhus

Every reasonable effort has been made to trace ownership and to obtain permission to reprint copyright material. The publishers would be pleased to have any errors or omissions brought to their attention so that they may be corrected in subsequent printings.

AV2 acknowledges Getty Images, iStock, Shutterstock, Newscom, and Alamy as its primary image suppliers for this title.